P9-BYS-161

D0015034

BUSY IN THE GARDEN

Poems by George Shannon

Pictures by Sam Williams

Greenwillow Books
An Imprint of HarperCollinsPublishers

For my godson, Santiago
—G. S.

For the Weeds
—S. W.

Busy in the Garden

Text copyright © 2006 by George Shannon

Illustrations copyright © 2006 by Sam Williams

All rights reserved. Manufactured in China. www.harperchildrens.com

Watercolor paints were used to prepare the full-color art.
The text type is Handysans.

Library of Congress Cataloging-in-Publication Data

Shannon, George.

Busy in the garden / by George Shannon ; pictures by Sam Williams.

p. cm.

"Greenwillow Books."

Summary: A collection of short poems and riddles about planting seeds, watching garden vegetables dance, and growing jack-o'-lanterns.

ISBN-10: 0-06-000464-9 (trade) ISBN-13: 978-0-06-000464-4 (trade)
ISBN-10: 0-06-000465-7 (lib. bdg.) ISBN-13: 978-0-06-000465-1 (lib. bdg.)

1. Gardens—Juvenile poetry. 2. Gardening—Juvenile poetry. 3. Children's poetry, American. [1. Gardens—Poetry. 2. Gardening—Poetry. 3. American poetry.]

I. Williams, Sam (date), ill. II. Title.

PS3569.H335B87 2005 811'.54—dc22 2003056863

First Edition 10 9 8 7 6 5 4 3 2 1

GREENWILLOW BOOKS

CONTENTS

SPRING ALARM!

Cock-a-doodle.

Do you see

the crocus in the sun?

Cock-a-doodle

dew! You know

that spring has now begun.

DIG IN

Dig a little.

Dig a lot.

Dig a brand-new garden spot.

Plant a little.

Plant a lot.

Plant the seeds and bulbs you bought.

Wait a little.

Wait a lot.

Wait much longer than you thought.

Pick a little.

Pick a lot.

Share the best bouquet you've got!

SEEDS

Do not forget
to get me lots,
or you'll not get
forget-me-nots!

11

GARDEN TIP

To grow enough to eat all year,

your seeds must be tiptop.

So plant both ends of old toy cars

and have a bumper crop!

A RIDDLE GARDEN

Mama planted summer hats.

Papa planted thread.

Sister planted ink stamps.

Brother planted bread.

MAY DAY

Fold a paper basket.

Flowers tucked inside.

Tiptoe. Knock, knock.

Quick, now run and hide!

BADMINTON, BAD!

Serve it fast.

Swoosh. Whack!

Zooming past.

Smack back!

Zing-ping.

Pong-bong.

Bing-boing.

Going-gone!

Landing on

the neighbor's lawn.

15

GARDEN MATH

Two seeds and two seeds,

that makes four.

But plant them in the ground,

and you'll get more!

BLUE RIBBON

To grow the size
that wins a prize,
it's always wise
to fertilize.

DANCING IN THE BREEZE

I went to the garden

to pick some peas.

Found them dancing

in the evening breeze.

The day was hot,

so I joined right in.

Tapped my toes

and began to grin.

Peppers in a polka
as the snow peas snapped.
Beans in a boogie
as the cabbage clapped.

Squash square dancing
with a cha-cha chard.
Watermelon waltzing
all around the yard.

Picked my supper
with the greatest ease—
everything swinging
in the dancing breeze.

LUCK

Green clover.

Bend over.

Count the leaves you see.

1-2-3.

1-2-3.

1-2-3-

4!

Pluck it.

Tuck it.

Save for luck.

Bend again

and search for more.

PICK A PETAL

Pick a petal—
Loves me.
Pick another—
Loves me not.
"Pick a Petal"
shows me—
A bald bouquet
is what I've got!

ZUCCHINI

Zucchini
meeny
miney
moe.
Plant a seed
and watch it grow.

Eeny
meeny
makes a lot.
Like a magic
cooking pot.

Eeny
meeny
munch a lot.
Zucchini every meal—
you've got:

22

Zucchini bread.
Zucchini spread.
Zucchini casseroles.

Zucchini pies.
Zucchini fries.
Zucchini dinner rolls.

Zucchini juice.
Zucchini mousse.
Zucchini jam and scone.

Zucchini hash
and succotash.
Zucchini
meeny
miney

MOAN.

WOULD YOU CARROT ALL TO DANCE?

CELERY dance? 1-2-3.

And SPINACH other round?

Feel the BEET! 1-2-3.

PEAS lift me off the ground.

What a PEAR! 1-2-3.

None better have BEAN found.

LETTUCE rest. 3-2-1.

My sweet potaTOES pound!

A RIDDLE PICNIC

Papa ate the root
and tossed the leaves.
Mama ate the leaves
and said "*Mine's* best!"
Brother ate the stem
and found no seeds.
Sister ate the seeds
and tossed the rest.

Sister=peas

Brother=celery

Mama=spinach

Papa=carrot

25

A CORNY RECIPE

Pick it outside.

Toss the outside.

Cook the inside
inside.

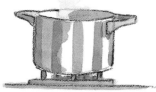

Eat the outside.

Toss the inside
outside once again.

BERRIES

When you're picking berries,

the hardest part is not

the picking, but the eating—

later on, *not* on the spot.

THE WAY TO PLAY CROQUET

Through the wicket
to the stick it
needs to click. It
isn't very hard.

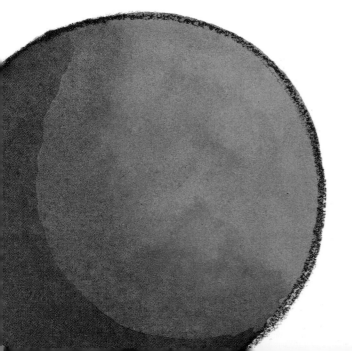

Till I block it,
swing, and knock it
far outside the yard!

SUPPER MATH

Four potatoes.

Five friends.

So how can I be fair?

Peel them, cook, and

mash them up.

Serve each an equal share!

STEW

Uproot a rutabaga.	Scrape a couple corncobs.
Turn a turnip up.	Wash a squash and chop.
Ferret out a carrot.	Toss them in the Crock-Pot.
Slice and dice them up.	Time to eat the crop!

HOE-DOWN!

It's time for a party.
Put your work hoe down.
Grab a tambourine
and erase that frown.
BANG-shake-a-jangle-o.
We're kicking up dirt!
All but the scarecrow—
What a stuffed shirt!

A BRIGHT IDEA

Plant a birthday candle
with every pumpkin seed,
and you'll grow jack-o'-lanterns.
Completely guaranteed!

GRASS

Hoe.

Sow.

Grow.

Mow.
Mow.

Mow.
Mow.

MOW.

Oh!

Snow!

Rest
and watch
the white yard
glow.

CORONATION

We'll pick a daisy
fresh with dew.
Pick some more,
and ivy, too.

Then split the stems
and link each through.
Crown you queen
and bow to you.